THIS AWESOME

SKETCHBOOK

BELONGS TO

DATE ______________

DATE ______________

DATE

DATE ______________

DATE

DATE

DATE

DATE

DATE ______________

DATE ____________

DATE ______________

DATE

DATE

DATE

DATE

DATE

DATE ______________

DATE

DATE ______________

DATE

DATE

DATE

DATE

DATE ______________

DATE

DATE

DATE

DATE ____________

DATE

DATE

DATE

DATE

DATE

DATE

DATE

DATE

DATE

DATE

DATE

DATE

DATE ______________

DATE

DATE

DATE

DATE

DATE ____________

DATE

DATE ____________

DATE ____________________

DATE

DATE ____________

DATE

DATE

DATE

DATE

DATE

DATE

DATE

DATE

DATE

DATE ____________

DATE

DATE ______________

DATE

DATE

DATE

DATE ______________

DATE ____________

DATE

DATE ______________

DATE ____________

DATE

DATE ____________

DATE

DATE

DATE ______________

DATE

DATE

DATE

DATE ______________

DATE

DATE ______________

DATE ______________

DATE

DATE

DATE

DATE

DATE

DATE

DATE ____________

DATE

DATE

DATE

DATE ________________

DATE

DATE ____________

DATE

DATE

DATE ______________

DATE ______________

DATE ______________

DATE ______________

DATE ______________

DATE

DATE

DATE ______________

DATE ______________

DATE ______________

www.ingramcontent.com/pod-product-compliance
Lightning Source LLC
Chambersburg PA
CBHW081006170526
45158CB00010B/2932
* 9 7 8 1 0 9 1 1 0 3 4 4 3 *